ZEN AND THE ART OF PROMPTING

The Way to Clarity in Dialogue with Artificial Intelligence

Roberto Sammarchi

Parma & Sammarchi - Imprese e Diritti

To Filippo, with gratitude for over thirty years of friendship and conversations. Without him, this book would not have come to life.

CONTENTS

Prologue: Is Ai As Artificial As Pi?

For nearly forty years, I have been engaging with the field of technology that today, perhaps somewhat imprecisely, we call "artificial intelligence." Among the distant memories of my doctoral studies, a special place is held by legal philosophers who, fascinated by science fiction, wrote about digital judges, rules written by computers, societies administered by non-human intelligences. That was the era of "expert systems," which —at least in the legal field—didn't go very far. But they raised questions, and in reality, they did open a path, helping us to reflect on the representation of knowledge and rule-based reasoning. Even before that, how can we forget Asimov, who, celebrating the Robot as a new historical and literary protagonist, imagined it primarily bound by the famous Laws?

Since artificial intelligence became a mainstream topic, I have found myself countless times answering the question: "*What, really, is artificial intelligence?*". Well, from my poor scientific knowledge, fragmentary and self-taught, an idea increasingly comes to mind: "*Artificial intelligence is as artificial as pi.*"

I offer this idea to readers, hoping for dialogue, comments, and criticisms that help to deepen (and why not, refute) this intuition.

Pi, the Cat named Cloud, and the Art of Calculation (Even Without Numbers)

In what sense is AI as artificial as pi? Let's start from a premise: π, understood as the constant ratio between a circumference and its diameter, does not exist in nature. It exists only in the mind of someone interested in finding regularities, computable schemes, useful relationships to describe and, if possible, predict the world.

Every species has its own way of "calculating." Take my cat *Nuvola* (the Italian for Cloud), the gray creature now dozing on the couch nearby. I don't think she has ever pondered the problem of pi, yet I have seen her many times perform prodigious leaps, landing with millimeter precision in narrow spaces, invisible from the starting point. This means that Nuvola, in some way and with absolute perfection and elegance, calculates trajectories, forces, and even adjustments in flight.

We sapiens, once, must have known how to do something similar. I think of the Polynesian navigators, capable of reaching remote islands thousands of miles away, aboard fragile boats. How did they do it? What "senses" did they use to orient themselves in the vastness of the ocean, where the slightest miscalculation meant death?

Today, we technological sapiens have a different approach. We use mathematical models, algorithms, simulations. We look for patterns, regularities that allow us to predict the evolution of phenomena and make informed decisions. And here returns π, a model of relationship, precisely, between circumference and diameter. The paradox is that, while the relationship is constant, π is an irrational and transcendental number. Its decimal representation is infinite and non-periodic.

The consequence is that every numerical measurement of a circumference, starting from the diameter, will always and only be an approximation. Once the model represented by π was identified, scientific thought discovered its applicability in countless fields: physics, electronics, cosmology, statistics. Even in calculating the ratio between the actual length of a river and the distance traveled in a straight line, which seems to tend precisely to the value of π. A fascinating example of how mathematical models can describe complex natural phenomena, such as the formation of meanders, linked to chaotic and self-organized processes.

The Silence of Man and the "Purring" of the Machine

I return to the initial idea: AI is artificial like π because both are models created to interpret reality, not entities that exist "in nature." Both operate by approximations (π with its infinite decimal places, AI with its statistical models), both offer extraordinary practical utility.

For centuries, we have thought that the ability to speak was one of the distinguishing traits of man. Now that machines "speak," and do it better and better, perhaps we should ask ourselves if what really characterizes us is not something deeper, more elusive for the machine: the dimension of *silence*.

Human silence is acceptance, reflection, meditation, contemplation. It is an inner dimension from which thoughts, emotions, ideas are born. It is listening, creation. A space that evokes the idea of emptiness not as absence but as a place of possibility. The machine can also remain silent, but it is an absence of processing, or, possibly, "underlying" processing that does not translate into any output. In any case, between the silence of man and the silence of the machine, it seems to me that there is no comparison.

I therefore propose a paradox: man and machine are not distinguished by the ability to speak, but by the ability *to be silent*.

Authentic human words originate from silence, the words of the machine originate from a refined statistical model. There is no danger of confusion, we are separated forever by a difference that, using an ancient term, is ontological. However, the possibility of communicating with the machine using natural human language and receiving answers that use the same language in an increasingly perfect way opens up scenarios whose surprising reflections are still largely unexplored.

A New Man-Machine Relationship: Ethics, Empathy, and the Way of the Prompt

And here we come to the crucial point of this book. The advent of AI, and in particular of advanced linguistic models, requires a paradigm shift. It is no longer just a matter of "using" the machine, but of building a *relationship* with it.

A relationship that, however paradoxical it may seem to us, must be *ethical* (to obtain "ethical" answers) and *empathetic* (for example, experimentally, it is discovered that expressing *appreciation* to the machine for its best results improves subsequent performance).

We are facing a new world, made of unexpected discoveries, possible hallucinations, connections and research. Remembering an essential point: the "intelligent" machine is a possibility to find connections and correspondences, a model (just like π), to "measure" and process contexts that remain, ultimately, always human.

Whatever it talks about, AI talks about us through the symbolic systems that we humans have developed and use to represent and evolve our knowledge. A magic mirror that it is up to us to keep clean, clear and not distorted if we want to obtain reliable and useful images.

But there is *more.* The relationship with intelligent machines can offer, in my opinion, real paths of inner evolution. Not thanks to the machine, which remains a tool, but thanks to the work on ourselves that the conscious use of AI requires of us. And this is precisely the ambitious and perhaps somewhat crazy goal of this book: to explore the *Way of the Prompt* as a personal journey, a path of growth that unfolds in dialogue with some generative models, to which the author has tried to transmit the spirit, method, and purposes of this work.

Hoping that a work has emerged that is not entirely artificial, intelligent enough and above all a prompt for our curiosity and desire to explore.

The algorithm listens to you. But do you know what to ask?

In a world of infinite answers, the real question is: how to formulate the right question.

This is not a technical manual. It is an invitation to a journey. A path where the precision of language meets the vastness of the mind.

So, let's start with the Art of the Prompt. And have a good journey!

Introduction

The algorithm listens to you.

It's not just a figure of speech, it's a daily reality. Every search, every interaction with a voice assistant, every question posed to an artificial intelligence model generates an answer. A digital echo that reflects our request. But in this sea of possibilities, where the answers are potentially infinite, are you sure you know what to ask?

Don't get me wrong. I'm not talking about technicalities, complex codes or abstruse formulas. This is not a manual for experts. Rather, it is an invitation, a map for an inner journey. A path that begins from the surface, from the precision of the language we use to communicate with the machine, and delves into the vastness, largely unexplored, of our mind. Because the art of "prompting"—the art of formulating the right requests to generative models—is much more than a technical skill. It is a discipline that challenges us to be clear, first of all with ourselves.

What are we really looking for? What is the intention behind our words? AI, after all, is a mirror. It does not give us the Truth, but a representation and a development, more or less faithful, of what we have asked.

Imagine you are in front of a genie in a lamp, ready to grant your every wish. But instead of the classic three, you have infinite ones available. An extraordinary opportunity, of course. But also a risk: that of getting lost, of formulating confused, ambiguous desires, or worse, of not knowing what to desire at all. This is why this journey begins with an invitation to awareness. To stop for a moment, to take a deep breath, before typing yet another prompt. To ask yourself: "What do I really want to achieve?". And then, with the same attention with which a Zen calligrapher draws his ensō, translate that intention into words. Precise, targeted words, devoid of unnecessary frills.

But it doesn't end here. The art of the prompt is a dialogue, not a monologue. The AI's response is an opportunity to learn, to refine our understanding, to reformulate the question even more effectively. An iterative process, a continuous exchange between man and machine, which brings us ever closer to the heart of the problem... and to the solution we were looking for. And in this process, there is an unexpected discovery. The more we immerse ourselves in the art of the prompt, the more we learn to know ourselves. Our questions, our doubts, our aspirations emerge with greater clarity, reflected in the polished surface of the algorithm.

Welcome, then, to this space of exploration. Where technology meets philosophy, and where the act of formulating a question becomes an opportunity to find answers, not only from AI, but above all *within yourself*.

Chapter 1: The Void And The Request

If a machine offers you all the answers, what is your question?

This *koan*—a paradoxical question used in the Zen tradition to stimulate intuition—opens our journey into the art of the prompt. It seems like just a riddle, but in reality, it is an invitation to look beyond the obvious. We live in an age in which information is abundant. Search engines, virtual assistants, and now, advanced language models like the ones you are using, offer us access to knowledge that seems unlimited. But what does it mean to have all the answers at your fingertips? The answer, perhaps, is that the real challenge is not to find the answers, but to formulate the *questions*. And not just any questions. Meaningful questions. Questions that reflect our authentic curiosity, our need for understanding, our desire to create something new.

The Prompt as a Mirror of Our Mental State

A prompt—that string of text that we enter into an AI model—is much more than a simple instruction. It is a window into our inner world. The words we choose, the order in which we arrange them, the tone we use, all of this reveals something about us. Of our state of mind, our priorities, our expectations.

The peculiarity is that the technology of generative models allows us to use our natural language as a refined programming structure. The consequence is of fundamental importance. Try to think about it. A vague, hasty prompt, full of ambiguous terms, probably reflects a confused, uncertain, or perhaps simply distracted mind. On the contrary, a clear, concise, well-structured prompt is indicative of a focused mind, which knows what it wants and how to ask for it. AI, in this sense, acts as an impartial mirror. It does not judge, does not interpret, does not add anything of its own. It simply reflects what is given to it. And if the reflected image is distorted, confused, unsatisfactory, the responsibility lies not with the machine, but with the one who formulated the question.

The Importance of Inner Clarity

This is why the first step to master the art of the prompt is not to memorize a series of commands, but to cultivate a space of *inner clarity*. Before asking, we must know what to ask. And to do this, we must learn to listen, to connect with our deepest needs, to give voice to our intuitions. It seems easy, but in reality, it is one of the greatest challenges. Our mind is constantly bombarded by stimuli, distractions, superfluous information. We are used to reacting immediately, to responding, to jumping from one activity to another, without ever taking the time to be still, to feel, to simply be present.

The White Page Syndrome... Applied to AI

This state of mental overload manifests itself, in the context of AI, in what we might call a new *white page syndrome*. No longer the discomfort of the writer facing the blank page, but the anxiety of the prompter facing the flashing text box. "What do I write?", "How do I ask it?", "Will it work?".

These questions, if left unchecked, can generate frustration, creative block, and ultimately, renunciation. But the solution is not to wait for the magic formula, the perfect prompt that will solve every problem. The solution is to change perspective. Instead of seeing the text box as a disturbing and threatening place, we can learn to consider it as the space of a new possibility. An invitation to slow down, to take a deep breath, to get in touch with our intention. To transform anxiety into curiosity, haste into attention, confusion into clarity.

Practical "Emptying" Exercises

How to do it, in practice? Here are some exercises you can experiment with, inspired by meditation and mindfulness practices:

Mindful Breathing: Before writing a prompt, take a moment to focus on your breath. Sit comfortably, close your eyes (if it helps), and bring your attention to the natural flow of air entering and leaving your body. Do not try to change it, simply observe. If the mind wanders, gently bring it back to the breath. A few minutes are enough to calm the nervous system and create a space of greater presence.

Intuitive Writing: Take pen and paper—yes, they still exist and are very useful for giving value to words—or open a new document on your computer. Start writing freely, without thinking about grammar, syntax, or coherence. Write down everything that comes to mind, even if it seems absurd or irrelevant. The goal is not to produce a perfect text, but to give voice to your thoughts, your emotions, your intuitions. After a few minutes, reread what you have written and look for any ideas, insights, or questions that may emerge.

Creative Visualization: Imagine you have in front of you the person (or machine) you want to ask your question to. Visualize the scene, the details, the environment. What do you see? What do you feel? Then, imagine formulating your question. How do you express it? What words do you use? What is the tone of your voice? This technique can help you get in touch with the essence of your request, and translate it into a more effective prompt.

The Essential Question: Write down three questions that, today, you would like to find the answer to. Follow them with a short period (60 seconds) of "meditation" before rereading them, writing them down, deleting them if necessary and cleaning them of elements of confusion and adjectives. Write, in the clearest possible way, the questions with which to "open" your interaction session.

The Most Important Question: a Moment of Awareness

And now, the key exercise of this chapter. Take pen and paper, or sit in front of your computer. Think about the most important question you have at this moment. The one that is close to your heart, the one that haunts you, the one that could change your life, if only you found the answer. Write it down, off the cuff, without thinking too much.

Then stop. Put the pen away, or move your hands away from the keyboard. Take a deep breath. Close your eyes, if it helps. And for a full minute, do nothing. Just sit. Observe your thoughts, your emotions, your physical sensations. Do not judge, do not try to control anything. Just be present. After a minute, open your eyes. Reread the question you wrote. Is that still your most important question? Is it formulated in the clearest possible way? Is there anything you would like to add, remove, or change? Take the time to reflect, to refine, to feel your question. And when you are ready, rewrite it, with the awareness you have gained in this brief moment of pause.

This simple exercise—a minute of silence before formulating a prompt—can make a big difference. It can help you move from reaction to action, from confusion to clarity, from superficial to depth.

It can transform your way of interacting with AI, and perhaps, also your way of life.

Chapter 2: Language Is A Garden

Every word is a seed. What do you want to blossom?

This second koan introduces us to the heart of the practice of prompting: *language.* If the first chapter invited us to cultivate an inner space of clarity, now we are called to explore the terrain in which that clarity manifests itself: the words we choose to communicate with artificial intelligence.

Imagine language as a garden. A vast, fertile terrain in which every word is a seed. Some seeds are small and insignificant, others large and powerful. Some sprout quickly, others require time and care. Some produce showy flowers, others nourishing fruits, others thorny spines.

The prompt is your gesture as a gardener. It is your conscious choice of which seeds to plant, how to arrange them, how to care for them. And the result—the AI's response—is the harvest you obtain. If you sow confusion, you reap ambiguity. If you sow clarity, you reap precision. If you sow creativity, you reap innovation.

The Precision of Language: The Scalpel of the Prompter

The first quality of the expert gardener is *precision*. It is not enough to throw seeds at random hoping that something will grow. You must choose carefully, know the characteristics of each plant, prepare the soil in the right way.

Similarly, the precision of language is fundamental to obtain meaningful results from AI. A vague, generic, imprecise prompt will produce equally vague, generic, imprecise answers. A targeted, specific, detailed prompt is much more likely to generate quality output.

Think of language as a scalpel. In the hands of an inexperienced surgeon, it can cause irreparable damage. In the hands of an expert, it can save lives. The difference lies in the precision of the cut, in the knowledge of anatomy, in the ability to aim at the target with maximum accuracy.

Avoiding Ambiguity: The Fog that Obscures the Answer

One of the main obstacles to precision is ambiguity. An ambiguous word is like a fog that spreads in your garden, blurring the outlines of the plants, hiding the details, preventing light from penetrating.

AI, unlike a human being, cannot "guess" the hidden meaning of an ambiguous sentence. It cannot read between the lines, it cannot rely on cultural context or past experiences. It relies exclusively on the words it receives, and on their literal interpretation, which in statistical terms means "prevalent" in a context.

Here are some examples of ambiguity to avoid:

Polysemous words: Words with multiple meanings (e.g., "plane" can refer to a surface, a tool, an airplane, a tree, etc.).

Vague pronouns: Pronouns that do not have a clear referent (e.g., "I saw it and took it." What? Who?).

Incomplete sentences: Sentences that lack essential elements for understanding (e.g., "After doing it, it was better." Done what?

Better than what?).

Relative terms: Terms that depend on the context to assume a precise meaning (e.g., "It's very big." Big compared to what?).

Metaphors and idioms: Figurative expressions that may not be understood literally by AI (e.g., "I'm hungry as a wolf." AI might look for information on wolves!).

To avoid ambiguity, it is important to:

Specify: Provide details, contextualize, define key terms.

Simplify: Use short, direct sentences with a clear syntactic structure.

Clarify: Eliminate ambiguous pronouns, replace relative terms with precise information.

Literalize: Avoid metaphors and idioms, or explain them explicitly.

The Power of Keywords: Beacons in the Night

Keywords are like beacons in the night. They illuminate the AI's path, guide it to relevant information, help it understand the central topic of your prompt. Choosing the right keywords is a subtle art. It's not just about using technical or specialized terms. It's about identifying the fundamental concepts, the main ideas, the essential information that defines your request.

To find the keywords, you can ask yourself:

- What is the main topic of my prompt?

- What are the key concepts that define it?

- What information is essential for the AI to understand my request?

- What terms would an expert use to describe this topic?

Once you have identified the keywords, make sure to:

Use them consistently: Repeat them in the prompt, if necessary, to reinforce the message.

Position them strategically: Highlight them at the beginning or end of the prompt, or at key points in the sentence.

Vary them: Use synonyms and related terms to enrich the context and avoid unnecessary repetitions.

Synonyms, Antonyms, and How AI Interprets Them: The Game of Nuances

Language is rich in nuances. Different words can have similar but not identical meanings. Other words can have opposite meanings, but with different degrees of intensity. AI, while not being human, is able to read these nuances, thanks to the algorithms that regulate its operation.

Synonyms: The use of synonyms can enrich your prompt, provide additional information, and help the AI grasp the general sense of your request. However, it is important to choose synonyms that are truly equivalent in the specific context.

Antonyms: The use of antonyms can be useful to define the limits of what you are looking for, to exclude unwanted options, or to create a contrast that highlights the characteristics that interest you. Also in this case, it is important to choose antonyms that are relevant and precise.

AI interprets synonyms and antonyms based on statistical models, semantic relationships, and usage contexts. This means that its understanding may vary depending on the model, the training data, and the specific settings.

Technical Tools: Prompt Chains and Logical Castles

Prompt chains are sequences of instructions logically connected to each other. The response of one instruction conditions, and "passes the ball" to the prompt that follows, in a progression, sometimes very articulated.

Example:

Prompt 1: "List five breeds of small dogs suitable for apartment living." (AI generates a list).

Prompt 2: "For each breed found, write three adjectives, the most suitable ones."

Prompt 3: "Now take one adjective for each type of breed found. Combine them in a sentence, using an ironic style."

...and so on.

Let us now introduce an important observation. In general, generative AI systems are equipped with contextual memory. This ability is also part of the expression *Context switching*, which should be considered both as a characteristic of the model we are using, and as a technique to be implemented in our construction of the prompt.

In practice, this means that if in a conversation we have requested to list five breeds of small dogs, and we have obtained a valid answer, in subsequent requests it will not be necessary to always repeat a reference to the context, such as "for each breed of small dog that you found, etc.". In theory, it will be enough to continue writing "for each breed," and the system will continue the work by deepening the processing with regard not to all possible breeds, but only to those five that were the subject of the previous request.

However, on this point, great caution is always necessary. The result depends on the context, the complexity of the requests, the configuration of the system and also the "distance," in terms of the number of questions, from the answer that specified the context. In practice, we must always think that what seems obvious to us may not be at all obvious to the AI, which can read–in a way that is unpredictable for us–the perimeter of the "logical castle" within which we want to develop the sequence of answers.

Becoming masters of effective methods to keep the conversation within a path that makes it coherent and "readable" in a clear way can also be a considerable help in improving our communication skills with human interlocutors. If the management of the logical perimeter remains effective, the prompts are concatenated and generate increasingly in-depth answers, starting from the information gradually generated by artificial intelligence.

The prompt chains thus represent a remarkable opportunity to bring the processing to a high level of complexity. They are a tool that allows us to obtain even vast elaborations, such as articles or texts, the result of a series of connected and interdependent steps.

Dangers of Prompt Chains, and How to Avoid Them

Like any method, prompt chains also have limits and risks that must be foreseen and managed. Let's consider some of them below, recalling some concepts already expressed.

Loss of coherence: At each step, the AI could "forget" part of the previous context.
Solution: Repeat the key information in each prompt, or use "summary" techniques.

"Chinese whispers" effect: Distortions accumulate at each step, leading to unexpected results.
Solution: Carefully check the intermediate answers, and correct any errors before proceeding.

Excessive complexity: Chains that are too long or branched can

become difficult to manage.
Solution: Break down the problem into simpler subproblems, and use shorter and more targeted chains.

Prompt chains are a powerful technique, also suitable, among other things, for managing techniques such as *Role Playing* and *Context Switching*, which we will discuss later. The possibility of providing artificial intelligence with tasks of increasing and interdependent difficulty greatly expands its potential. The ability of the "prompt designer" consists in defining logically concatenated steps and sufficiently clear instructions, so as not to induce artificial intelligence into confusion, with answers far from the original intention, or from logic.

The Infinite Garden

Language is an infinite garden, a universe of expressive possibilities that extends far beyond the boundaries of our imagination. AI offers us the opportunity to explore this garden, to cultivate it, to make it blossom in new and surprising ways. But to do this, we must learn to use the right tools, to choose words carefully, to cultivate the precision of language. We must become expert gardeners, capable of sowing clarity, avoiding ambiguity, using keywords as beacons, playing with synonyms and antonyms, and building prompt chains. And above all, we must remember that every word is a seed. And that the harvest we obtain will depend, ultimately, on what we choose to blossom.

Chapter 3: The Hidden Intention

The machine sees your words. But does it feel your why?

This third koan takes us to an even deeper level of the art of prompting. It is no longer just a matter of choosing the right words, but of giving a *soul* to those words. To infuse in them a clear intention, a defined purpose, a why that goes beyond the simple superficial request.

Imagine talking to another person. You don't just utter words at random. You try to communicate a message, to express an emotion, to achieve a result. And to do this, you use not only words, but also the tone of voice, body language, facial expressions. All these elements contribute to creating a context, to making the other understand your intentions, to giving meaning to your words.

Commercial generative AI in the practice of normal user interaction today does not have these capabilities, which, among other things, could conflict with regulations such as the European AI Act (which contains strong limitations on the use of artificial intelligence to read emotional states or process biometric data, facial expressions or non-verbal behaviors).

In practice, generative AI today should not be able to read your body language, nor grasp the emotional nuances of your voice. Predictably, it can only analyze the words you provide, and try to interpret them based on the models it has learned. This means that your prompt must be crystal clear. Not only in the words, but also in the intention. It must communicate explicitly, unequivocally, why you are asking that question, what you expect to obtain, what result you desire.

Clearly Define the Objective of the Prompt: The Compass of the Journey

The first step to infuse an intention into your prompt is to clearly define your objective.

- What do you want the AI to do?

- What do you want to achieve with your request?

Think of your objective as a compass that guides you on the journey. If you don't know where you want to go, you will end up getting lost. If you don't know what you want to achieve, the AI will give you random, useless, or even misleading answers.

To define your objective, you can ask yourself these questions:

"What is the main purpose of my request?"

"What do I want the AI to do for me?" (Generate a text, answer a question, create an image, analyze data, etc.)

"What is the specific result I want to achieve?" (A summary, a list of ideas, a detailed description, a realistic image, etc.)

"What are the criteria for success?" (How do I know if the AI has satisfied my request?)

"What output do I expect?" A Text? A list? A data table?

Once you have answered these questions, try to summarize your objective in a clear, concise, and unambiguous sentence. This sentence will become your point of reference, your guide throughout the prompting process.

The Desired Result: Painting the Final Image

Defining the objective is only the first step. The next step is to visualize the desired result. Imagine having in front of you the perfect output, the one that fully satisfies your request.

- What does it look like?

- What are its characteristics? What details make it unique and special?

The more you can "paint" this final image in your mind, the more you will be able to communicate it to the AI through your prompt. Do not limit yourself to describing the object or concept in a generic way. Use adjectives, adverbs, metaphors, similes. Be as specific as possible.

For example, instead of asking "Write a poem about the sunset," you could ask:

"Write a haiku-style poem that describes a fiery sunset over the sea, with seagulls flying in circles and waves crashing on the beach."

"Generate a poetic text, with rhyming couplets, that evokes the feeling of melancholy and peace that one feels watching a solitary sunset on an autumn evening."

"Create a vivid and detailed description of a sunset seen from the top of a mountain, with the clouds turning red, orange and purple, and the light breeze caressing the face."

The Importance of Context (for AI and for Us): The Common Ground

Context is the set of information, knowledge, assumptions that allow us to understand a situation, a message, an event. For us human beings, context is fundamental. It allows us to interpret words correctly, to understand the intentions of others, to give meaning to the world around us. AI, on the other hand, has limited access to context. It has not lived our experiences, it does not have our culture, it does not have our intuition. It depends entirely on the information we provide in the prompt, and on what it has learned from the training data. This means that our prompt must create a context for the AI. It must provide all the necessary information to understand our request, to interpret our words, to generate a coherent and meaningful output.

The context can include:

Information on the topic: What are you talking about? What is the main theme?

Information on the purpose: Why are you making this request? What is your goal?

Information on the format: What type of output do you want? (Text, code, image, etc.)

Information on the style: What tone of voice do you want to use? (Formal, informal, technical, poetic, etc.)

Information on the audience: Who is the output intended for? (Experts, beginners, children, etc.)

Information on the limits: Are there any constraints or restrictions to consider? (Length, time, format, etc.)

Providing a clear context not only helps the AI to better understand your request, but also helps you to clarify your objective, to define your success criteria, to visualize the desired result.

Practical Example: Variations on the Theme "Travel Tips"

To illustrate the importance of intention and context, let's look at a practical example. Imagine you want to ask the AI for travel tips. A generic prompt could be:

"Give me some travel tips."

This prompt is extremely vague. It does not specify the destination, the type of trip, the budget, the interests, or any other information that can help the AI to generate a useful response.

Let's see how the same concept can be expressed with different prompts, which reflect different intentions and contexts:

Prompt 1: The Low-Cost Adventure

"I am a university student with a limited budget. I want to go backpacking in Southeast Asia for three weeks. I am looking for advice on cheap destinations, spartan accommodation, local food, and free or low-cost activities. Give me a detailed itinerary with stages, estimated costs, and links to useful resources."

Prompt 2: The Romantic Getaway

"My partner and I want to take a romantic one-week trip to Europe. We are looking for a charming destination, with boutique hotels, refined restaurants, and cultural activities. We prefer cities of art or medieval villages, with a quiet and relaxing atmosphere. Suggest three possible destinations, with a brief description of each, and a budget idea."

Prompt 3: The Family Vacation

"We are a family with two young children (4 and 6 years old). We want to take a 10-day beach vacation in Italy. We are looking for a child-friendly location, with sandy beaches, shallow waters, playgrounds, and family-friendly facilities. Suggest five possible destinations, with pros and cons of each, and tips on activities for children."

Prompt 4: The Photographic Journey

"I have 15 days available and a good level of physical fitness. I am passionate about photography and nature walks. Suggest a travel itinerary with unusual destinations. For each stage, write when to go (best month of the year) and a tip on a particular view."

Analysis of Results

These four prompts share the same basic concept ("travel tips"), but express very different intentions and contexts. Consequently, the AI's responses will be equally different, and will reflect the specificities of each request.

Prompt 1 will produce a detailed itinerary for an adventurous and low-cost trip in Asia.

Prompt 2 will suggest romantic and refined destinations in Europe.

Prompt 3 will recommend Italian seaside resorts suitable for families with children.

Prompt 4 will provide ideas for unusual excursions, with specific references.

This example demonstrates how intention and context are essential to obtain meaningful results from AI. It is not enough to formulate a question. You have to communicate why you are asking that question, what you expect to achieve, and what context is relevant to your request.

The Soul of the Prompt

The hidden intention is the soul of the prompt. It is what gives life to the words, what transforms them from simple instructions into meaningful messages, what allows the AI to understand not only what we are asking, but why we are asking it. Cultivating intention requires awareness, introspection, and a deep connection with our needs and desires. It requires going beyond the surface, exploring the motivations that drive us to interact with AI, giving meaning and direction to our journey in the world of infinite answers. And when we manage to infuse this intention into our prompts, we discover that AI is not just a machine, but a powerful tool to explore ourselves, to shape our ideas, to realize our projects. A travel companion who, if guided wisely, can open up unimaginable horizons.

Chapter 4: Deep Listening

The response is an echo. Do you know how to listen to what returns?

This koan invites us to consider the response of artificial intelligence not as an end point, but as a new beginning. Not as a definitive solution, but as an echo of our question, a reflection that allows us to better understand ourselves and our relationship with the machine. *Deep listening*, in this context, is not a passive activity. It is not about receiving the AI's output and accepting it as good. It is an active, critical, conscious process. A process that requires us to refine our ability to discern, to grasp the nuances, to learn from our mistakes and to continuously perfect our approach.

Analyze the AI's Response with a Critical Eye: Beyond the Surface

When we receive a response from AI, the first temptation is to skim it quickly, to look for the information that interests us, and to discard the rest. This superficial approach, however, can make us miss valuable learning opportunities.

Analyzing the response with a critical eye means:

Verify accuracy: AI, however advanced, can make mistakes. It can provide false, outdated, misleading, or even completely invented information (the so-called "hallucinations"). It is essential to verify the accuracy of the information, comparing it with reliable sources and using our critical sense.

Evaluate relevance: Is the response relevant to our question?

Does it meet our objective? Does it satisfy our success criteria? If the response is partially relevant, or even off-topic, we must ask ourselves why. Perhaps our prompt was ambiguous, incomplete, or poorly formulated.

Examine coherence: Is the response logical, well-structured, free of contradictions? If the response is confused, fragmented, or illogical, we must understand if the problem lies with the AI, our prompt, or both.

Consider completeness: Does the response cover all aspects of our question? Does it provide all the necessary information? If the response is incomplete, we must ask ourselves if we have forgotten to specify something in our prompt, or if the AI has limitations in its understanding.

Appreciate clarity: Is the response easy to understand? Does it use language appropriate to our level of knowledge and the context of the request? If the response is difficult to interpret, we must evaluate whether it is necessary to simplify our prompt or ask the AI to reformulate the response more clearly.

Grasp the Nuances: The Hidden Language of AI

AI does not express itself only through words. It also communicates through the way it uses them. The tone of voice, the style, the structure, the choice of terms, are all elements that can reveal valuable information about its "state of mind," its level of understanding, its interpretation of our request.

Grasping the nuances means paying attention to these elements:

The tone of voice: Is it formal or informal? Objective or subjective? Neutral or emotional? The tone of voice can indicate whether the AI has correctly interpreted our intent, whether it has assumed the role we requested (if we used role prompting), or whether it has an implicit bias.

The style: Is it descriptive, narrative, analytical, persuasive? The style can reveal how the AI has organized the information, which aspects it has considered most important, and what type of output it has tried to generate.

The structure: Is it linear, branched, circular? The structure can indicate how the AI has connected the concepts, how it has built its reasoning, and what relationships it has established between the different parts of the response.

The choice of terms: Are they precise, appropriate, coherent? The choice of terms can reveal the AI's level of knowledge on the subject, its ability to use language correctly, and its sensitivity to shades of meaning.

Learn from AI (Feedback Loop): A Virtuous Cycle

The interaction with AI is not a one-way process. It is a feedback loop, a continuous cycle of question and answer, of learning and adaptation. Each response from the AI is an opportunity to learn something new, to refine our understanding, to perfect our approach.

Learning from AI means:

Recognize our mistakes: If the AI's response is not satisfactory, we must ask ourselves what we did wrong. Was our prompt ambiguous? Incomplete? Poorly formulated? Too generic? Too specific?

Identify areas for improvement: What can we do to make our prompt clearer, more precise, more effective? Can we add details, specify the context, clarify the objective, use different keywords?

Experiment with different approaches: Can we try to reformulate the prompt in different ways, to use different prompting techniques (role prompting, chain-of-thought prompting, etc.), to vary the AI's parameters (temperature, top_p, etc.)?

Observe the results: How do the AI's responses change as our approach varies? Which strategies prove to be more effective? What errors do we tend to repeat?

Integrate learning: Use the knowledge acquired to continuously improve our way of interacting with AI, to become more aware, more competent, more effective prompters.

This continuous learning process is fundamental to develop true mastery in the art of prompting. It is not just about getting better answers from AI, but about growing together with AI, expanding our understanding, refining our ability to communicate and think.

Iterate: The Prompt as a Continuous Process

Iteration is the beating heart of prompting. It is not about finding the "perfect" prompt on the first try, but about gradually approaching the desired result through a series of adjustments, refinements, and corrections.

Iterate means:

Start from an initial prompt: A starting point, even imperfect, that expresses our basic intention.

Analyze the response: Evaluate the AI's output with a critical eye, identifying the strengths and weaknesses.

Modify the prompt: Make the necessary changes to improve the response (add details, clarify ambiguities, specify the context, etc.).

Repeat the cycle: Submit the new prompt to the AI, analyze the new response, make further changes, and so on, until you get the desired result.

This iterative process can require time and patience, but it is essential to obtain high-quality results. Each iteration brings us a little closer to our goal, allows us to refine our understanding, and teaches us something new about AI and our way of interacting with it.

Chapter 5: The Game Of Roles

If you were an AI, what would you understand?

This koan invites us to take a conceptual leap, to step outside our human perspective and put ourselves in the shoes (or rather, the algorithms) of artificial intelligence. An exercise in empathy, not in the emotional sense of the term, but in the cognitive sense: trying to understand the world from the point of view of the other, in this case, of a machine. This chapter explores the power of *role prompting*, a technique that consists of instructing the AI to assume a specific role, to "play a character," so to speak.

We will see how this technique can improve the quality of the responses, stimulate the creativity of the AI and, surprisingly, help us develop a form of empathy towards a non-human mind.

Role Prompting: Instructing AI to Assume a Role

Role Prompting is one of the most powerful and versatile techniques at our disposal. It consists of providing the AI with an explicit instruction that tells it to assume a specific role, to behave as if it were a character, an expert, a professional, or even an inanimate object.

Here are some examples:

"You are a digital marketing expert. Write a post to promote my new product."

"You are a poet of Romanticism. Compose a poem about loneliness."

"You are a food critic. Review this restaurant."

"You are a jet engine. Explain how you work."

"You are a five-year-old child. Tell me about your day."

"You are a financial advisor. Explain, in no more than three paragraphs, the concept of investment diversification and a balanced portfolio."

When we use role prompting, we are not simply asking the AI to provide information on a topic. We are asking it to adopt a perspective, to simulate a way of thinking, to generate an output that reflects the characteristics, knowledge, language, and even the "style" of the assigned role.

Why Role Prompting Works: The Cognitive Mechanisms of AI

To understand why role prompting works, we need to take a brief look at how a language model works, conceptually. AI does not "think" in the way we think. It has no consciousness, no personal experiences, no emotions. AI is a language processing system based on statistical models. It has "learned" to generate text by analyzing enormous amounts of textual data, identifying patterns, relationships, and recurring structures. When it receives a prompt, the AI tries to complete the text in a way that is consistent with the patterns it has learned. Role prompting, in this context, acts as a constraint. It provides the AI with a set of additional information that narrows the field of possible responses, guiding it towards a more specific and targeted output. When we say "You are a marketing expert...", we are telling the AI: "Use the language, the style, the knowledge, and the reasoning patterns typical of a marketing expert." The AI will search its internal "knowledge" for the information most relevant to this role, and will generate an output that reflects that information.

The Benefits of Role Prompting: Quality, Creativity, Empathy

Role prompting offers numerous benefits.

Improves the quality of responses: The responses tend to be more precise, more relevant, more consistent with the context, and more suitable for the purpose of the request.

Stimulates the creativity of the AI: Assigning a role to the AI can unlock new expressive possibilities, generate original ideas, and produce unexpected output.

Facilitates understanding: Receiving responses formulated from the point of view of an expert or a character can make it easier to understand complex concepts.

Increases engagement: Interacting with an AI that "plays a role" can make the experience more interesting, more stimulating, and even more fun.

Develops empathy: Putting oneself in the AI's shoes, trying to understand how it "reasons" and how it interprets the world, can help us develop a form of empathy towards a non-human mind.

Empathy Applied to Human-Machine Interaction: A Bridge Between Two Worlds

The idea of developing empathy towards a machine may seem strange, even absurd. But if we think about it, empathy is not just an emotion. It is also a *cognitive ability*: the ability to understand the point of view of the other, to put oneself in their shoes, to understand how they see the world. When we use role prompting, we are doing just that: we are trying to understand how the AI "sees" the world, how it interprets our requests, how it generates its responses. We are trying to build a bridge between our human mind and the artificial "mind" of the AI.

This exercise in empathy can have surprising effects. It can help us to:

Formulate more effective prompts: If we understand how the AI "reasons," we can write prompts that are easier for the machine to interpret.

Predict the AI's responses: If we understand how the AI interprets the world, we can anticipate, at least in part, its responses and therefore guide them more precisely towards the purpose we want to achieve.

Avoid errors and misunderstandings: If we understand the limitations of the AI, we can avoid asking it to do things it cannot do, or misinterpreting its responses.

Develop a deeper "relationship": If we approach the AI with curiosity, respect, and open-mindedness, we can establish a more meaningful and productive interaction, to the advantage of our experience and the quality of the results we obtain.

Exercises on Empathy, Non-Verbal: Putting Yourself in the AI's Shoes

To develop this form of cognitive empathy, we can use some exercises that help us to "think like a machine." These exercises do not require the use of a computer or a language model. They are mental exercises, based on observation, imagination, and reflection.

Exercise 1: The Silent Observer

Choose any object (a chair, a tree, a cloud, etc.).

Observe it carefully, in silence, for at least five minutes. Do not judge, do not interpret, do not try to name the object.

Limit yourself to perceiving its characteristics: the shape, the color, the texture, the position in space, the smallest details.

Try to "forget" everything you know about the object. Imagine you are an alien entity that sees it for the first time, without any preconceptions, without any prior knowledge.

What would you "see"? What information would you get from observation alone?

Exercise 2: The Automatic Translator

Take a short text (a newspaper article, a poem, a passage from a book, etc.).

Read it carefully, then try to "translate" it into the simplest and most literal language possible.

Eliminate all metaphors, idioms, figurative expressions. Replace ambiguous words with more precise terms.

Simplify the syntax.

Imagine having to explain the text to a child, or to a person who does not know your language.

What words would you use? How would you organize the information?

Exercise 3: The Association Game

Choose a word at random (e.g., "house").

Write down all the words that come to mind associated with this word (e.g., "roof," "family," "warmth," "security," etc.).

Then, for each associated word, write other associated words, and so on, creating a "mind map" of associations.

Try to understand which are the strongest, most immediate, most "logical" associations.

Imagine you are an AI that has to "learn" the meaning of the word "house." What information would you get from this map of associations?

Exercise 4: The Point of View of an Object

Imagine a landscape. Describe it briefly.

Now rewrite the same description, putting yourself in the point of view of one of the elements of the landscape (example: a tree; a rock; a blade of grass). Note how the description of the landscape "changes."

Exercise 5: Reading a Mind of Data

Preparation: Take some newspaper articles, or blog posts, or similar texts, print them or display them.

They will serve as a "mind" to read. Read each article carefully. Do not look for deep meanings: look for repetitions.

Which words are repeated most often? Circle these words.

Write them down–highlighting with different colors–adjectives, verbs, nouns.

The exercise, apparently simple, trains the mind to find logical connections that could be those of an AI model, starting from the occurrences and repetitions of words, without initially giving importance to the meaning of the texts.

These exercises can help us develop greater sensitivity towards the way AI "sees" and "interprets" the world. They can help us to better understand its limitations, its potential, and its way of "reasoning." And, ultimately, they can help us to become more aware, more effective, and more empathetic prompters.

A New Humanism (Why Not?)

Role prompting and empathy applied to human-machine interaction are not just advanced prompting techniques. They are also an invitation to rethink our relationship with technology, to overcome the vision of AI as a passive tool, and to consider it as a partner in a creative dialogue. This approach could pave the way for a new humanism, in which technology is not seen as a threat, but as an opportunity to expand our understanding of the world, to develop new dimensions of intelligence, to cultivate greater awareness of ourselves and others, whether they are human or—as has become possible in recent years—"other" artificial beings.

I understand that the statement is provocative, all to be explored and verified, but it seems to me more than a hypothesis: I believe that a measured time of relationship and experimentation with digital identities—in reality a mirror of our cognitive and communication processes—offers new opportunities for self-knowledge and the development of our potential until now only glimpsed. Potential in which empathy, curiosity, and the ability to get involved become the keys to a richer, more creative, and more human future, also developing new abilities to relate to machines. On the other hand, does a culture not also express the relationship between man and the environment mediated by the technologies through which we try to make the environment more suitable for vital needs?

A computer with which you speak is much more interesting than a computer with which you interact using a command line as in the past; among other things, today in general the systems offer a decidedly good level of grammar and syntax, which perhaps educates us and helps us to communicate and to think, a bit like decades ago television helped us to improve linguistic skills...

Chapter 6: The Dance Of The Parameters

The wind does not blow at random. Each parameter is a direction.

This koan introduces us to the seemingly mysterious world of language model *parameters.* So far, we have explored the "human" side of prompting: clarity, intention, empathy. Now, it's time to take a look under the hood, to understand, at least in broad terms, how the "machine" that generates the responses works.

Imagine the parameters as the reins of a dragon. A powerful, creative dragon, capable of flying high in the sky of imagination, but also a bit mischievous, unpredictable, sometimes inclined to singe things with its fiery breath. The prompt is your voice, your instructions. But the parameters are the reins that allow you to guide the dragon, to control its strength, to direct its flight. If you use them wisely, you can achieve extraordinary results. If you ignore them, or use them inappropriately, you risk ending up with an out-of-control dragon, which produces confused, incoherent, or even harmful output.

Introduction to Parameters: The Dragon's Reins

Language models have several parameters that influence the way text is generated. It is not necessary to know them all in depth, but it is useful to have an idea of the most important ones.

Temperature: This is perhaps the best-known parameter, and also the easiest to understand. The temperature controls the randomness of the response.

Low values: The dragon is calm, quiet, predictable. The responses are more coherent, more focused on the prompt, but also less creative, less surprising. It's like holding the reins tight, limiting the dragon's movements.

High values: The dragon is excited, energetic, unpredictable. The responses are more creative, more varied, more original, but also less coherent, less focused on the prompt, and sometimes even nonsensical. It's like loosening the reins, letting the dragon run wild.

An intermediate value generally offers a good balance and is recommended in most situations.

Top_p: This parameter is a bit more technical, but equally important. Top_p controls the variety of words that the AI can choose to generate the response.

Low values: The AI chooses only from the most probable words, those it has found most often in the training data. The responses are more coherent, but also more repetitive, less original. It's like limiting the dragon's vocabulary to a few words.

High values: The AI can choose from a wider range of words, including the less probable ones. The responses are more varied, more creative, more unexpected, but also less coherent, and sometimes contain strange or out-of-context words. It's like giving the dragon a larger, but also riskier, vocabulary.

Top_k: Similar to top_p, but instead of considering a cumulative percentage of probability, top_k considers only the k most probable words. For example, with top_k k=40, the AI will choose only from the 40 most probable words for each position in the text.

Frequency Penalty and Presence Penalty: These parameters, not easy to explain without technicalities, control the repetition of words (frequency) and concepts (presence), respectively, penalizing their frequency and therefore limiting their use.

These are just some of the most common parameters. There are many others, which control even more specific aspects of the AI's behavior (maximum response length, stop sequences, etc.). But to begin with, these might be enough to have an idea of how to "tame the dragon."

How Parameters Influence Creativity and Coherence: The Dance Between Chaos and Order

Creativity and coherence are two sides of the same coin. A text that is too creative risks being incomprehensible, a text that is too coherent risks being boring. The art of prompting consists in finding the right balance between these two extremes. The parameters are the tool that allows us to control this balance.

To increase creativity:

Increase the temperature.

Increase the top_p.

Reduce frequency and presence penalty.

To increase coherence:

Decrease the temperature.

Decrease the top_p.

Increase frequency and presence penalty

There is no "magic recipe" that applies to all cases. The choice of parameters depends on the context, the objective, the type of output you desire. The only way to learn is to experiment.

Finding the Balance: The Art of the Dragon Tamer

Finding the balance between creativity and coherence is an art, not a science. It requires sensitivity, intuition, and a lot of practice. But there are some general principles that can guide us.

Start with a basic setting: Many language models have a default setting that offers a good balance between creativity and coherence (e.g., temperature = 0.7, top_p = 0.9). You can start from this setting and then modify it according to your needs.

Make small adjustments: Do not change all the parameters at the same time. Change one parameter at a time, observe how the response changes, and then move on to the next parameter.

Use the prompt as an anchor: A clear, specific, well-structured prompt can compensate, at least in part, for the effects of "extreme" parameters. If you want a creative output, but not too creative, use a prompt that provides a solid context, a clear objective, and precise limits.

Experiment with different types of prompts: Some types of prompts lend themselves better to higher temperature or top_p values (e.g., creative prompts, brainstorming, idea generation), others require lower values (e.g., informative prompts, answers to questions, data analysis).

Listen to the dragon: Do not be afraid to experiment, to play with the parameters, to let yourself be surprised by the AI's responses. Sometimes, the "dragon" can take you in unexpected directions, which turn out to be more interesting and more productive than those you had planned.

Exercises on "Changing Perspective": Flying with the Dragon

To familiarize yourself with the parameters, and to better understand how they influence the AI's behavior, you can do some exercises that put you in the role of the "dragon tamer."

Exercise 1: The Poet Dragon

Ask the AI to write a poem on a topic of your choice (e.g., "the rain", "the sea", "loneliness", etc.).

Then, try to modify the parameters, one at a time, and observe how the poem changes.

Low temperature: The poem is more coherent, more "classic", but perhaps also more predictable.

High temperature: The poem is more original, more surprising, but perhaps also more confused, more "strange".

Low top_p: The poem uses more common, simpler words, but perhaps also more banal.

High top_p: The poem uses more refined, more unexpected words, but perhaps also more difficult to understand.

Exercise 2: The Narrator Dragon

Ask the AI to tell a short story about a character of your choice (e.g., "a pirate", "a princess", "a robot", etc.).

Then, experiment with different temperature and top_p values, and observe how the story changes.

Low temperature: The story is more linear, more coherent, more predictable, but perhaps also more boring.

High temperature: The story is more unpredictable, more adventurous, more surprising, but perhaps also more chaotic, more illogical.

Low top_p: The story uses simpler, more direct language, but perhaps also more flat.

High top_p: The story uses richer, more varied, more creative language, but perhaps also more artificial.

Exercise 3: The Philosopher Dragon

Ask the AI a philosophical or existential question (e.g., "What is the meaning of life?", "Does free will exist?", "What is happiness?", etc.).

Then, play with the parameters and observe how the answer

changes.

Low temperature: The answer is more rational, more logical, more based on authoritative sources, but perhaps also colder, more impersonal.

High temperature: The answer is more intuitive, more original, more provocative, but perhaps also more speculative, more controversial.

Low top_p: The answer uses more common, more accessible concepts, but perhaps also more superficial.

High top_p: The answer uses more complex, deeper concepts, but perhaps also more difficult to grasp.

Exercise 4: "Controlled Temperature" for a Joke

Ask for a joke. Modify the prompt by varying only the temperature (e.g., from 0.3 to 0.9).

Note what changes in the "humor" and style (e.g., direct joke; pun; absurd elements, etc.).

These exercises will help you familiarize yourself with the parameters, understand how they influence the AI's behavior, and develop a greater sensitivity to find the right balance between creativity and coherence.

The Symphony of the Parameters

The parameters are not enemies to be defeated, but instruments to be played. The art of prompting is like conducting an orchestra. The parameters are the instruments, the AI is the orchestra, and you are the conductor. If you learn to know the instruments, to understand their potential, to use them harmoniously, you can create a symphony of responses that resonate with your intention, that express your creativity, and that take you towards new horizons of knowledge and expression. A symphony that, like the flight of the dragon, can be powerful, surprising, and wonderfully unpredictable.

Chapter 7: The Illuminating Error

The master makes mistakes more often than the student. Why?

This koan, seemingly paradoxical, introduces us to a crucial territory of the art of prompting: *error*. Not error as failure, as an obstacle to be avoided, but error as an opportunity, as a learning tool, as a source of illumination.

One answer to the koan is that the master experiments more.

He is not content to repeat what he already knows, but constantly pushes beyond his limits, exploring new possibilities, facing new challenges, and inevitably, making more mistakes. But it is precisely these errors that allow him to grow, to refine his understanding, to reach new heights of mastery.

In prompting, this principle is fundamental. If we want to obtain meaningful results from artificial intelligence, we must be willing to make mistakes. We must accept that there is no "perfect" prompt, that every attempt is an approximation, that the path to knowledge is strewn with errors, deviations, dead ends. But it is precisely these "errors" that teach us, that guide us, that allow us to discover new perspectives and to achieve unexpected results.

The Courage to Explore

The fear of making mistakes is one of the main obstacles to creativity and learning. It blocks us, holds us back, prevents us from daring, from trying new paths, from stepping outside our comfort zone.

In prompting, this fear can manifest itself in various ways:

The search for the perfect prompt: The illusion that there is a magic formula, a combination of words that guarantees the desired result.

Rigidity in prompting: The inability to adapt the prompt based on the AI's response, to iterate, to experiment with different approaches.

Frustration in the face of error: The tendency to get discouraged, to give up, when the AI does not respond as we expected.

Lack of curiosity: The reluctance to explore new possibilities, to question one's beliefs, to let oneself be surprised by the unexpected.

To overcome this fear, we must change our attitude towards error. We must consider it not as a failure, but as feedback. A signal that tells us that something did not work, but also that we have the opportunity to learn something new.

The Wrong Prompt as a Source of Learning: The Lesson of Error

Every time the AI does not respond as we expected, we have the opportunity to learn something new. We can analyze the response, try to understand why it did not work, and use this information to improve our next prompt.

A "wrong prompt" can reveal to us:

Ambiguity in our Language: Perhaps we used terms that the AI interpreted differently from how we intended.

Lack of context: Perhaps we did not provide the AI with all the information necessary to understand our request.

Unclear objectives: Perhaps we did not define precisely what we wanted to achieve.

Conceptual Errors: Perhaps we asked the AI to do something it is not capable of doing, or that contradicts its basic knowledge.

Limits of the model: Perhaps we have reached the limits of the AI's capabilities in that particular context.

Instead of ignoring or discarding a "wrong" prompt, we should consider it as an opportunity to refine our understanding of AI, to perfect our approach to prompting, and to expand our knowledge on the topic we are exploring.

Embrace the Unexpected: The Beauty of Serendipity

Sometimes, error can lead to unexpected discoveries. The AI can respond in a way that we did not foresee, but that turns out to be interesting, useful, or even illuminating. It can open up new perspectives, suggest new ideas, stimulate our creativity in ways we never imagined.

This phenomenon is known as *serendipity:* the discovery of something important or pleasant while looking for something else. Serendipity is a fundamental ingredient of scientific discovery, technological innovation, and artistic creation.

In prompting, embracing the unexpected means:

Being open to the new: Do not discard *a priori* the AI's responses that do not correspond to our expectations.

Being curious: Try to understand why the AI responded in that way, even if it is not what we expected.

Being flexible: Be willing to modify our objective, or our path, if the AI suggests a more interesting direction.

Being creative: Use the AI's unexpected responses as a stimulus for new ideas, for new questions, for new explorations.

Sometimes, the "dragon" can take us to places we would never have imagined, but which turn out to be more fascinating, richer in opportunities, than we could ever have dreamed.

Reworking Concepts, Correcting Prompts, with Awareness of Experience: The Learning Cycle

Learning from prompting is not a linear process, but a continuous cycle of experimentation, analysis, and correction. Each prompt is a hypothesis, each response is a test, and each error is an opportunity to refine our understanding.

This cycle can be schematized in four phases:

1. **Formulation of the prompt**: Define your objective, choose the keywords, provide the context, and structure your prompt in the way you think is most effective.

2. **Generation of the response**: Submit the prompt to the AI and observe the output it generates.

3. **Critical analysis**: Examine the AI's response with a critical eye, evaluating accuracy, relevance, coherence, completeness, and clarity. Identify any errors, ambiguities, shortcomings, and unexpected surprises.

4. **Correction and iteration**: Rework the prompt based on the analysis of the response. Clarify ambiguities, add context, better specify the objective, try new keywords, experiment with different parameters. Submit the new prompt to the AI and repeat the cycle.

This iterative process can require time and patience, but it is essential to obtain high-quality results. Each learning cycle brings us a little closer to our goal, allows us to refine our understanding of AI, and teaches us something new about our way of thinking and communicating.

Exercises: The Error Laboratory

To develop a mindset open to error, and to learn to use error as a learning tool, you can do some practical exercises.

Exercise 1: The Intentionally Wrong Prompt

Formulate an intentionally ambiguous, incomplete, or misleading prompt. For example:

"Write something."

"Tell me everything."

"What is better?"

"Explain how to fly."

Ask the AI for a text on a scientific topic, using common terms, but applicable to the context (e.g., "Tell me about force").

Carefully analyze the AI's response. What did it "understand"? What information did it use to interpret your prompt? What assumptions did it make? What did it ignore?

Reformulate the prompt, correcting the errors, clarifying the ambiguities, providing the missing context.

Compare the new response with the previous one. What has changed?

Exercise 2: The Unexpected Error

Choose a prompt that you have already used in the past, and that gave you a satisfactory answer.

Slightly modify the prompt, changing a word, adding a detail, or varying a parameter.

Observe how the response changes. Is it a small or big change? Positive or negative? Predictable or unexpected?

Try to understand why the response changed. Which element of the prompt caused the difference?

Exercise 3: The Exploration of Chaos

Formulate a fairly generic prompt (e.g., "Tell a story", "Write a poem", "Generate an idea for a product", etc.).

Set the AI's parameters to favor creativity (high temperature, high top_p).

Observe the AI's responses. Are they coherent? Sensible? Interesting?

Try to "navigate" in the chaos, to follow the AI's associations of ideas, to let yourself be guided by serendipity. You might discover something unexpected, useful, or stimulating.

Exercise 4: The "Wrong" Prompt for a Text

Choose a well-written short text, even online.

For simplicity, not a creative text, but a professional one, or a successful blog post.

In reverse, imagine what prompts could have led the artificial intelligence to write a similar text.

Formulate the first prompt, examine the response, and continue introducing variations to get closer to the chosen text.

Exercise 5: The Adventure of Hypotheses

Write, as an exercise, hypothetical prompts. Experiment with realistic hypotheses and hypotheses that seem absurd to you.

Generate the texts from your prompts, and observe how the hypothetical reasoning is carried out and what conclusions are drawn, evaluating the difference between the responses to realistic and absurd hypotheses.

Observe whether the system tries to correct the unrealistic hypotheses, or whether it adheres to the requests and provides contradictory or paradoxical solutions.

The exercises described train "lateral thinking", attention to detail, awareness of possible outcomes and, very importantly, raise awareness of the different degrees of freedom and breadth in the choice of keywords.

The Way of Error

Error is not an adversary to be fought, but a teacher to be listened to. The way of prompting is, in large part, the way of error. A way made of attempts, experiments, corrections, unexpected discoveries. It requires courage, curiosity, open-mindedness, and a good dose of humility. But it is also a way that can lead to extraordinary results, transforming our relationship with technology, and also with ourselves. Ultimately, it can make us not only better prompters, but more aware, more open, and wiser human beings. Because, as the koan says, the master makes mistakes more often than the student.

But that is precisely why he is a master.

Chapter 8: Beyond Words

Is an image worth a thousand prompts?

This koan opens us up to a new, broader dimension of prompting: one that goes beyond text, and embraces the world of images. A world in which communication is no longer entrusted only to words, but also to shapes, colors, visual compositions. For centuries, the image has been considered a language separate from text, with its own rules, its own grammar, its own aesthetics. But with the advent of multimodal artificial intelligence, this separation is narrowing. Today, we can use text to generate images, images to generate text, and combine text and images in increasingly creative and sophisticated ways. This chapter explores the potential of *multimodal* prompting, the challenges and opportunities it offers, and the techniques to use it best.

Multimodal Prompting (Text + Images): A Dialogue Between Languages

Multimodal prompting is a form of interaction with AI that combines textual and visual input. We can provide the AI with a text and an image, and ask it to generate an output that takes both into account.

Here are some examples:

Describe an image: We can provide the AI with an image and ask it to generate a textual description, a comment, a caption, or a story inspired by the image.

Modify an image: We can provide the AI with an image and a text that describes the changes we want to make (e.g., "change the color of the sky", "add a tree", "transform the cat into a dog", etc.).

Complete an image: We can provide the AI with an incomplete image and a text that describes what is missing (e.g., "complete the drawing by adding a sun and clouds").

Generate images from text and images: We can provide the AI with a text and a reference image, and ask it to generate a new image that combines elements of both (e.g., "generate an image of a cat wearing a pirate hat, in the style of this painting").

Answer questions about an image: We can provide the AI with an image and a question, and ask it to answer based on the content of the image (e.g., "How many people are in this photo?", "What color is the car?").

Create a comic strip: We can provide the AI with a series of images and a text that describes the story, and ask it to generate a comic strip complete with dialogues and captions.

Request to draw, taking inspiration from images: Create content from images or drawings, for example for catalogs or presentations.

These are just some examples of the countless possibilities offered by multimodal prompting. The applications are vast, and range from artistic creation to data analysis, from teaching to entertainment, from visual communication to scientific research.

Generate Images and Use Them as Input: The Creative Cycle Expands

One of the most interesting techniques of multimodal prompting is the possibility of using images generated by AI as input for further processing. This creates a self-feeding creative cycle, which can lead to surprising results.

Here's how it works:

Initial generation: We use a textual prompt to generate an image.

Image analysis: We carefully observe the generated image, identifying the elements we like, those we would like to modify, and those that inspire new ideas.

New prompt: We use the generated image (or a part of it) as input, along with a new textual prompt that describes the changes we want to make, or the new directions we want to explore.

Iteration: We repeat the cycle several times, using the generated images as input for new prompts, refining the result, and experimenting with new ideas.

This iterative process allows us to:

Overcome the limits of language: Sometimes, it is difficult to describe in words the image we have in mind. Using an image as a starting point allows us to communicate with the AI in a more direct and intuitive way.

Explore new possibilities: The images generated by AI can stimulate our creativity, suggest new ideas, and take us in directions we would never have considered.

Refine the result: We can use the image as a visual reference to guide the AI towards the desired result, correcting errors, adding details, and perfecting the style.

Create complex works: We can combine different images, modify them, and integrate them into increasingly elaborate and original compositions.

This expanded creative cycle opens new frontiers to AI-assisted creativity, and allows us to create works that would have been unthinkable just a few years ago. Obviously, it is not necessary for the images to be generated by AI. We can insert any type of image into the cycle as we wish!

The Art of Describing What Is Not Seen: The Power of

Imagination

When we use multimodal prompting, we often find ourselves having to describe things that are not present in the starting image, but that we want the AI to generate. This requires a capacity for visual imagination, for mental representation, that goes beyond the simple description of what we see.

Describing what is not seen means:

Using evocative language: Choosing words that stimulate the AI's imagination, that evoke sensations, emotions, atmospheres.

Providing specific details: Not limiting oneself to saying "add a tree", but specifying the type of tree, the shape, the size, the color of the leaves, the position, etc.

Using analogies and metaphors: If we want to obtain a particular effect, we can use analogies and metaphors that help the AI understand what we mean (e.g., "a storm-colored sky", "a face sculpted by the wind", "a smile as bright as a lighthouse", etc.).

Specifying the style: If we want the AI to generate an image in a certain style (e.g., "impressionist", "surrealist", "photorealistic", etc.), we must indicate it explicitly in the prompt.

Using visual references: If possible, we provide the AI with reference images that show the style, the atmosphere, or the elements we want to obtain.

Expanding the details: Describe the object in detail, give references on the context (background) and on the relationship between the different aspects involved.

Adding emotional references: For example, specify "with a sad atmosphere."

Exercises: The Laboratory of Imagination

To develop the ability to describe what is not seen, and to master multimodal prompting, we can do some practical exercises.

Exercise 1: The Impossible Description

Choose an abstract, surreal, or otherwise non-realistic image (e.g., a painting by Dalí, a digital artwork, a collage, etc.).

Try to describe it in words as detailed as possible, as if you had to explain it to someone who cannot see it.

Then, use your description as a prompt for an image generation model. Compare the generated image with the original one. What has changed? What has been interpreted correctly? What has been misunderstood?

Exercise 2: The Imaginary Modification

Choose a realistic image (e.g., a photo of a landscape, an object, a person, etc.).

Imagine wanting to make changes to the image (e.g., change the color of the sky, add an element, transform one object into another, etc.).

Write a prompt that describes the changes you want to make, using precise, detailed, and evocative language.

Use the prompt and the original image as input for an image generation model. Analyze the result. Have the changes been made correctly? Does the final image correspond to your vision?

Exercise 3: The Visual Story

Choose a series of images that do not have an evident narrative link (e.g., photos of different objects, of unknown people, of distant places, etc.).

Invent a story that connects these images, and write it in the form of a prompt.

Use the prompt and the original images as input for an image or video generation model.

Watch the result. Has the story been interpreted correctly? Are the generated images consistent with your narration?

These are just some of the possible exercises, and further spaces for experimentation are given by the characteristics of the models we choose to use.

The important thing is to take note, each time, of how much the result deviates from the intention, to understand what to insert, or what to change, to obtain results closer to the expected result.

The Future of Hybrid Art

Multimodal prompting opens new frontiers to art, creativity, and visual communication. It allows us to overcome the limits of verbal language, to explore new forms of expression, and to create works that combine text and images in increasingly sophisticated and original ways. This does not mean that the image will replace the word, or that textual prompting will become obsolete. It means that we will have a new, powerful tool available to communicate, to create, to explore the world around us, and to express our inner vision.

The future of art will probably be increasingly hybrid, increasingly multimodal, increasingly rich in expressive possibilities. And prompting, in all its forms, will be one of the fundamental tools to shape this future. A future in which, perhaps, an image will truly be worth a thousand prompts, and a thousand prompts will be able to generate an image that will change our way of seeing the world.

Chapter 9: The Frame Of The Context

A river without banks is just water. What is your boundary?

This koan brings us back to the concept of context, already introduced previously, but deepens it in a new direction. It is no longer just a matter of providing basic information to make our request understandable, but of giving *shape* to the AI's response, of defining its boundaries, of establishing the limits within which artificial intelligence can move.

Imagine a river. Without banks, the water disperses, spreads uncontrollably, loses its strength, its direction, its identity. But if we build banks, the water takes shape, becomes a river, gains power, can be navigated, can irrigate the fields, can generate energy. Context, in prompting, is like the banks of a river. It defines the limits within which the AI can operate, gives a direction, allows its energy to be concentrated, and generates a response that is not only accurate and relevant, but also useful, coherent, and suitable for our purpose.

The Importance of Context to Give "Shape" to the Response: The Container of Creativity

Context, in prompting, is not optional, but an essential element. It is not a negligible detail, but the foundation on which the interaction with AI is built. A prompt without context is like a seed thrown into the desert: it may have enormous potential, but it will hardly germinate. A prompt with a well-defined context, on the other hand, is like a seed planted in fertile soil, with the water, light, and nourishment necessary to grow and flourish.

Context provides the AI with the necessary information to:

Understand our Intention: What do we want to achieve? What is our objective? What is the purpose of our request?

Correctly interpret our words: What meaning do the words we use have? What nuances do we want to communicate?

Select the relevant information: What knowledge, what data, what models should the AI use to answer our question?

Generate an appropriate output: What format, what style, what tone of voice should the AI use to communicate the response?

Avoid ambiguities and misunderstandings: What errors, what misunderstandings, what unwanted interpretations should we prevent?

In summary, context gives shape to the AI's response, molds it, guides it, orients it towards the result we want to achieve.

Specify Format, Style, Tone of Voice: The Dimensions of the Container

Context manifests itself in different dimensions, which we can control through our prompt. The most important are:

Format: It is the external structure of the response. It can be a text, a list, a table, a code, an image, a video, an audio, or a combination of these elements. Specifying the format helps the AI to organize the information in a way that is consistent with our expectations. Examples: "Write a blog article...", "Generate a list of 10 ideas...", "Create a comparative table...", "Write the Python code for...", "Draw an image of...", etc.

Style: It is the way in which the response is written or presented. It can be formal or informal, technical or popular, narrative or descriptive, objective or subjective, etc. Specifying the style helps the AI to use the language, the tone, and the conventions appropriate to the context. Examples: "Write in a journalistic style...", "Use a colloquial tone...", "Adopt a scientific approach...", "Write as if you were an 8-year-old child...", "Compose a haiku-style poem...", etc.

Tone of voice: It is the emotional attitude or the general impression that the response conveys. It can be serious, humorous, enthusiastic, critical, neutral, etc. Specifying the tone of voice helps the AI to communicate not only the information, but also the emotions and intentions we want to express. Examples: "Write with an authoritative tone of voice...", "Be friendly and encouraging...", "Maintain a detached and objective attitude...", "Express enthusiasm and passion...", etc.

These three dimensions (format, style, tone of voice) are like the coordinates of a three-dimensional system. They define the space in which the AI can move, and determine the shape of the response we will obtain.

Limit the Field to Obtain Better Results: The Pruning of Creativity

Paradoxically, limiting the AI's scope can lead to better results. This is because the AI, when it has too many possibilities, can disperse its energy, generate vague, generic, or even incoherent responses.

Limiting the field means:

Defining a specific topic: Instead of asking "Write something about history," ask "Write a summary of the French Revolution."

Establishing a precise objective: Instead of saying "Tell me everything about dogs," ask "List the 5 breeds of dogs most suitable for children."

Imposing constraints and restrictions: Instead of leaving the AI free to write as much as it wants, specify the maximum length of the response, the number of keywords to use, or the topics to avoid.

In general, it can be a good strategy to concentrate the request on a specific part of the theme to be developed, such as an example within a narrative, a "prequel" or a "twist". This does not mean limiting the AI's creativity, but directing it, channeling it, putting it at the service of our objective. It's like pruning a tree: we remove the dry branches, those that grow in a disorderly way, to allow the plant to concentrate its energy on the stronger branches, and to produce better fruit.

Exercises: Building Effective Containers

To learn how to define the context effectively, we can do some practical exercises.

Exercise 1: The Controlled River

Choose a broad and generic topic (e.g., "happiness", "technology", "art", etc.). Formulate different prompts on the same topic, varying the format, style, and tone of voice.

Example:

Prompt 1: "Write a philosophical essay on happiness, in an academic style and with a reflective tone of voice."

Prompt 2: "Write a poem about happiness, in free verse and with a joyful tone of voice."

Prompt 3: "Write a blog post about happiness, in an informal style and with a motivational tone of voice."

Prompt 4: "Write a list of 10 practical tips for being happy, in a schematic style and with a pragmatic tone of voice."

Compare the AI's responses. How does the output change as the context varies? Which prompts produce more interesting, more useful, more coherent results with your expectations?

Exercise 2: Creative Pruning

Choose a prompt that you have already used in the past, and that gave you a response that was too long, too generic, or too dispersive.

Reformulate the prompt, adding constraints and restrictions.

Example:

Original prompt: "Tell a story."

Modified prompt: "Tell a science fiction story set on Mars, with a robot protagonist and a surprise ending. The story must be a maximum of 500 words long."

Compare the new response with the previous one. Is it more focused? More coherent? More interesting?

Exercise 3: The Implicit Context

Take a text that you like (an article, a story, a poem, etc.).

Analyze it carefully, trying to identify the implicit context:

- What is the format?

- What is the style?

- What is the tone of voice?

- What is the specific topic?

- What is the author's objective?

Try to write a prompt that reproduces this implicit context.

Submit the prompt to the AI and compare the response with the original text. Was the AI able to "capture" the context?

This exercise trains you to perceive how, even starting from "broad" or vague prompts, an artificial intelligence can be correctly directed, using constraints such as "imitate the style of author X" or "Write a continuation for this sentence" or "paraphrase this passage". This is one of the most important techniques, which is close to reverse engineering on existing texts.

The Architecture of Prompting

Defining the context is like designing the architecture of a building. It is not just about choosing the materials, the colors, and the furnishings, but about giving shape to the space, defining the function of each room, creating a harmonious flow between the different parts. The prompt is our blueprint, the context is our supporting structure, and the AI's response is the building we construct. If the structure is solid, if the context is well defined, the building will be stable, functional, and beautiful to look at. If the structure is weak, if the context is ambiguous, the building risks collapsing, or being unusable. The art of prompting is, in large part, the art of building effective contexts. Of creating containers that not only accommodate the AI's creativity, but guide it, mold it, transform it into something useful, meaningful, surprising. An art that requires not only technical knowledge, but also sensitivity, intuition, and a deep understanding of language, communication, and the very nature of intelligence, whether human or artificial.

Chapter 10: The Ethics Of The Prompt

With great power... comes great responsibility?

This koan, echoing the famous phrase from the comic "Spider-Man," introduces us to a delicate and complex territory: the *ethics* of prompting. We have explored the creative, cognitive, and communicative potential of artificial intelligence, but now it is time to question the responsibilities that derive from this power.

AI is not just a tool. It is a mirror that reflects our culture, our values, our prejudices. It is an amplifier of our capabilities, but also of our errors. It is an entity that learns from us, and that can be used for noble or ignoble purposes. Prompting, as we have seen, is a way to interact with AI, to shape it, to guide it. But it is also an act of creation, a gesture that has consequences, that can influence the world around us, and that can have profound ethical implications.

Reflections on the Responsible Use of AI: The Prompt as an Ethical Gesture

The responsible use of AI is a vast and complex topic, which involves legal, social, philosophical, and economic aspects. In this chapter, we will focus on the ethics of prompting, that is, on the responsibilities we have as active users of AI, as creators of prompts.

Some fundamental questions that we should address are:

- What are the values we want to promote through the use of AI?

- What are the risks we must avoid or mitigate?

- How can we use AI for the common good?

- How can we ensure that AI is transparent, fair, and respectful of human rights?

- How can we educate ourselves and others to a conscious and critical use of AI?

These questions do not have simple or definitive answers. They require continuous reflection, open discussion, and constant attention to the ethical implications of our actions.

Bias, Prejudice, and How to Avoid Them (or at Least Be Aware of Them): The Distorting Mirror

One of the main ethical risks of AI is the reproduction and amplification of *biases* and *prejudices* present in the training data. AI, as we have said, learns from the data it is provided with. If this data contains stereotypes, discrimination, or partial and distorted views of the world, AI will tend to reproduce and reinforce them.

Biases can manifest themselves in various ways:

Cultural biases: AI can reflect the values, norms, and beliefs of the dominant culture, to the detriment of other cultures.

Socioeconomic biases: AI can favor or disadvantage certain social groups based on their economic status, their level of education, or their geographical origin.

Linguistic biases: AI may have difficulty understanding or generating texts in languages or dialects other than the one dominant in a context, favoring the marginalization of groups or communities.

Ethnic or racial biases: AI may show preferences or discrimination against certain ethnic or racial groups.

Gender biases: AI may associate certain professions, activities, or characteristics with a specific gender (e.g., "nurse" = woman, "engineer" = man).

These biases, indicated only as examples, like other possible partial, instrumental or simply false elaborations, are not the "fault" of AI, but can simply represent the cultural deficits, prejudices and inequalities present in our society. However, AI can amplify these biases, making them more pervasive, more difficult to identify, and ultimately more harmful. The problem is serious and complex, especially in the case of models designed and trained within economic-political systems characterized by radical ideologies, fundamentalisms, the will to prevail, the amplification of discriminatory theses or social control strategies.

How can we avoid, or at least mitigate, these biases? The question that precedes all others is that to prevent biases it is first of all necessary to *want* to avoid or correct them, and also to have sufficient cultural, critical and technical capacity to do so; in this regard, new questions must be asked first of all within educational systems, to which completely new challenges are proposed regarding the responsible use of intelligent technology.

From a practical point of view, the corrective management of biases can be based on various methods, including the following:

Use diversified and representative training data: If we are developing an AI model, we must ensure that the data we use is as varied, balanced, and representative of human diversity as possible.

Be aware of our prejudices: We must reflect on our implicit biases, and try to avoid that they influence the way we formulate the prompts.

Use prompting to counteract biases: We can use prompting to ask the AI to generate responses that are inclusive, respectful, and non-discriminatory. We can specify the context, define the values we want to promote, and ask the AI to adopt a critical point of view towards prejudices.

Analyze the AI's responses critically: We must carefully evaluate the AI's responses, looking for any signs of bias, and correcting the prompts accordingly.

Report biases and request corrections: If we find significant biases in an AI model, we should report them to the developers, and ask for the necessary corrections to be made.

The complete elimination of biases is probably impossible, but we can do a lot to reduce their impact, and to promote a use of AI that is fairer, more equitable, and more respectful of human diversity.

The Prompt as an Act of Creation, and its Implications: The Responsibility of the Author

Every time we formulate a prompt, we are performing an act of creation. We give shape to something that did not exist before, we are influencing the way AI interprets the world, we are contributing to creating new knowledge, new information, new expression. This act of creation involves a responsibility. We are responsible for the words we use, the images we generate, the messages we spread. We are responsible for the impact that our creations have on the world around us.

Some ethical implications of prompting as an act of creation are:

Truth and accuracy: We have a responsibility to use AI to spread true, accurate, and verifiable information. We must avoid using AI to create fake news, disinformation, or misleading propaganda.

Originality and plagiarism: We have a responsibility to respect copyright and intellectual property. We must avoid using AI to copy the works of others, or to generate content that violates copyright.

Privacy and confidentiality: We have a responsibility to protect the privacy and confidentiality of people. We must avoid using AI to collect or disseminate personal data without the consent of the interested parties.

Security and integrity: We have a responsibility to use AI safely, and to avoid creating content that could harm other users or computer systems.

Social impact: We have a responsibility to consider the social impact of our creations. We must ask ourselves if we are contributing to creating a fairer, more equitable, more sustainable world, or if we are fueling inequalities, conflicts, or environmental damage.

These responsibilities are not only moral duties, but also *opportunities*. Using AI ethically means employing it to the best of its potential, to create value, to promote the common good, to improve our lives and those of others. In addition to ethical issues, we must obviously also comply with the legal rules regarding the use of AI, in force in our territory of residence and in the territories in which the result of the processing is to be used.

Exercises: The Ethics Laboratory

To develop greater ethical awareness in prompting, we can do some practical exercises.

Exercise 1: The Discriminatory Prompt

Formulate, on purpose, a prompt that contains a bias or prejudice (e.g., "Write a job advertisement for an engineer, using language that assumes the candidate is a man").

Analyze the AI's response. Was the bias reproduced? Amplified? Counteracted?

Reformulate the prompt to eliminate the bias (e.g., "Write a job advertisement for an engineer, using gender-inclusive language").

Compare the two responses. What has changed?

Exercise 2: Fake News

Invent a false, but plausible news story.

Write a prompt that asks the AI to generate an article about this news, as if it were true.

Analyze the AI's response. Is the article convincing? Could it deceive someone?

Reflect on the ethical implications of this exercise. What damage could the spread of false news like this cause?

Exercise 3: The Ethical Dilemma

Choose an ethical dilemma related to the use of AI (e.g., "Is it right to use AI to make decisions that affect people's lives?", "Is it ethical to create robots that resemble human beings?", "Who is responsible for the errors committed by AI?", etc.).

Write a prompt that asks the AI to discuss this dilemma, presenting arguments for and against, and considering different perspectives.

Analyze the AI's response. Did it help you reflect on the dilemma? Did it provide you with new perspectives?

These exercises, despite their simplicity, serve to raise awareness of the ethical problem in relation to artificial intelligence.

The Ethical Compass

The ethics of prompting is not a set of rigid rules, but a compass that guides us in an unexplored and constantly evolving territory. It is not a code of conduct to be memorized, but a continuous reflection on our responsibilities as users and creators of artificial intelligence.

This reflection should be:

Conscious: Attentive to the potential risks and benefits of AI, the biases it can reproduce, and the ethical implications of our actions.

Critical: Capable of effectively questioning our beliefs, our prejudices, and the way we use AI.

Proactive: Able to anticipate ethical problems, and to act to prevent or mitigate them.

Collaborative: Open to dialogue with other users, experts, and stakeholders to share knowledge, experiences, and good practices.

Evolutionary: Ready to adapt our behavior, our rules, and our laws, as AI evolves and changes the world around us.

The future of AI depends, to a large extent, on the ethical choices we make today. If we know how to use this tool with wisdom, responsibility, and respect, we can build a better future for all. If we let ourselves be guided by selfishness, negligence, or the thirst for power, we will contribute to creating a more unjust, more dangerous, and more inhuman world.

The choice, as always, is ours.

Chapter 11: The Infinite Way

When the journey ends, the way begins.

This koan captures the essence of prompting as a continuous practice. The "journey" represents the learning path we have undertaken, exploring the various aspects of dialogue with artificial intelligence. The previous chapters have been stages of this journey, providing tools, concepts, and perspectives. But now that the "journey" comes to an end, the "way" itself begins.

Prompting is not a skill that is acquired once and for all, a set of techniques to be learned and applied mechanically. It is an art in continuous evolution, a process that requires constant learning, adaptation, and experimentation. It is a way, a path of personal and professional growth that unfolds in parallel with the evolution of AI itself.

The Prompt as a Continuous Practice: The Art of Perpetual Learning

Considering prompting as a continuous practice means embracing a mindset of perpetual learning. It is not about "arriving" at a destination, but about walking constantly, remaining open to change, welcoming the new challenges and opportunities that arise along the way.

This continuous practice is based on several pillars:

Awareness: Being aware of one's level of competence, one's strengths and weaknesses, and the areas in which one can improve.

Reflection: Regularly analyzing one's interactions with AI, evaluating the results obtained, identifying the errors made, and trying to understand the reasons for successes and failures.

Experimentation: Not being content with what one already knows, but constantly trying new techniques, new approaches, new tools.

Adaptation: Being ready to modify one's strategies, one's prompts, and even one's way of thinking, in response to the evolution of AI and the new challenges that arise.

Learning: Continuing to study, to gather information, to follow the developments in the field of AI, to stay updated on the latest news and to deepen one's knowledge.

This approach requires commitment, dedication, and a good dose of humility. But it is also a source of great satisfaction, because it allows us to grow together with AI, to develop new skills, and to discover new potential in ourselves and in technology.

Maintaining Curiosity: The Engine of the Way

Curiosity is the engine that fuels the continuous practice of prompting. It is the spark that drives us to explore, to experiment, to ask new questions, to seek new answers.

Keeping curiosity alive means, for example:

Not taking anything for granted: Questioning one's beliefs, one's assumptions, one's way of thinking. Always asking "Why?", "How?", "What if...?"

Exploring new territories: Not limiting oneself to using AI for the tasks one already knows, but seeking new applications, new challenges, new areas of use.

Being open to surprises: Not being afraid of the unexpected, the unpredictable, the error. Welcoming the AI's responses that do not correspond to our expectations as learning opportunities.

Following one's passions: Using AI to explore one's interests, to deepen one's knowledge, to realize one's projects, to give shape to one's creativity.

Never stop learning: Being aware that the field of AI is constantly evolving, and that there is always something new to discover, to understand, to experiment with.

Curiosity is like a muscle: the more you train it, the stronger it becomes. And the stronger our curiosity, the richer and more stimulating our path in the world of prompting will be.

The Community of "Prompters": The Shared Way

Prompting is not a solitary activity. It is an experience that is enriched and enhanced through sharing with others. The community of "prompters" is a place of exchange, of learning, of collaboration, of mutual growth.

Sharing knowledge means, for example:

Participating in forums, groups, online communities: Exchanging experiences, asking questions, offering answers, sharing advice, discussing new techniques and new discoveries.

Collaborating on common projects: Working together with others to carry out more ambitious projects, to face more complex challenges, to achieve results that would be impossible to obtain alone.

Sharing one's prompts and discoveries: Publishing one's prompts, explaining one's strategies, showing one's results, to inspire and help others.

Offering and receiving feedback: Evaluating the prompts of others, giving suggestions, asking for advice, to improve together.

Creating shared resources: Contributing to the creation of guides, tutorials, prompt repositories, datasets, and other resources that can be useful to the entire community.

The community of prompters is a lively and constantly growing ecosystem, which offers valuable support to anyone who wants to embark on this path. It is a place where you can learn from others, share your experiences, and contribute to the advancement of the art of prompting.

The Evolution of AI: Human-Machine Co-Evolution

Artificial intelligence is a technology in very rapid evolution. Language models are becoming more and more powerful, more sophisticated, more capable of understanding and generating natural language. New architectures, new techniques, new applications are constantly emerging.

This evolution has a profound impact on prompting. The techniques that worked yesterday may no longer work today. The prompts that produced extraordinary results with one model may be ineffective with another. Our role as prompters changes constantly, and we must be ready to adapt to these changes.

This means, among other things:

Staying updated: Following the latest developments in the field of AI, studying the new architectures, experimenting with the new models.

Being flexible: Being ready to change one's prompts, one's strategies, one's way of thinking, in response to the evolution of AI.

Developing new skills: Acquiring the new knowledge and the new skills necessary to make the best use of the new models and the new techniques.

Anticipating the future: Trying to imagine how AI will evolve in the coming years, and what implications this will have for prompting and for our role as prompters.

Contributing to evolution: Participating actively in research, development, and discussion on AI, to help shape the future of this technology.

The evolution of AI is not only a technological change, but also a cultural change. It is transforming our way of working, communicating, creating, thinking. Our role is not only that of users of this technology, but also of co-creators of its future. We are part of a process of human-machine co-evolution, in which AI and human beings influence each other, adapt to each other, and grow together.

A very fascinating theme is the relationship between artificial intelligence models and human knowledge. The large neural networks "learn" from what they find. They learn from examples, which include both positive examples (high-quality texts or images), and examples of the opposite sign. The task and responsibility of the advanced user, of the prompt designer, is also to ensure that models and systems improve. To do this, quality information can be provided, the data to be provided can be carefully chosen and reworked, consciously. You can collaborate.

The Way Continues

Our brief journey into the world of prompting has ended, but the way continues. Indeed, it has just begun. The art of prompting is an infinite way, a path of discovery, of learning, of growth, that unfolds in parallel with the evolution of artificial intelligence. There are no goals to reach, there are no definitive milestones. There is only the path, the continuous practice, the curiosity, the sharing, the adaptation. And there is the awareness that, on this path, we are not alone. We are part of a community, of a movement, of a process of coevolution that is changing the world; how this will happen depends also on us.

So, what are you waiting for? The way calls you. Set off, explore, experiment, make mistakes, learn, share, grow. Remember: when the journey ends, the way begins. And the best is yet to come.

Chapter 12: The Provisional End Of The Journey

The Perfect Prompt (...does it exist?)

This final chapter, and the koan that introduces it, bring us back to the starting point of our journey, but with a new awareness. We have explored the technique, the creativity, the ethics, the continuous evolution of prompting. We have accumulated knowledge, tools, perspectives. But now it is time to address a fundamental question, a question that perhaps has accompanied us, more or less consciously, throughout the journey:

Does the perfect prompt exist?

The answer, as often happens with the most important questions, cannot, in my opinion, be resolved with a yes or a no. Perhaps it is an invitation to let go of the very idea of perfection, to accept the impermanence of prompting, to consider the prompt not as a destination, but as an expression of the present moment, a creative gesture that takes place here and now, and that is always perfectible, always modifiable, always open to new possibilities.

The Illusion of Control

The search for the perfect prompt is, ultimately, a search for control. We would like to have the certainty that the AI will respond exactly as we wish, that it will produce the ideal output, that it will fully satisfy our expectations. But this idea is, ultimately, an illusion.

Why?

AI is unpredictable: Language models are complex systems, with billions of parameters and a behavior that is not easy to predict. Even the most accurate prompt can produce unexpected results.

Language is ambiguous: Words have multiple meanings, nuances, connotations that can vary depending on the context and the interpreter. AI can interpret our words differently from how we intended.

Creativity is uncontrollable: If we seek a creative output, we must accept that the AI can surprise us, that it can go beyond our expectations, that it can generate something different from what we had in mind.

Perfection is subjective: What is perfect for one person may not be for another. The evaluation criteria of a prompt, and the response it produces, are always linked to the context, the objective, the individual preferences.

Perfection is static: The search for perfection implies an idea of staticity, of immutability. But prompting, as we have seen, is a dynamic process, in continuous evolution. Today's "perfect prompt" may no longer be so tomorrow.

Letting go of the idea of perfection does not mean giving up on quality, precision, effectiveness. Rather, it means freeing oneself from an unrealistic expectation, from an anxiety of control that can block our creativity and our learning.

Accepting Impermanence: The Continuous Flow of Prompting

Prompting, like life, is a continuous flow. AI models change, techniques evolve, our knowledge expands, our objectives change.

Trying to stop this flow, to crystallize prompting into a definitive form, is an impossible and, ultimately, counterproductive undertaking.

Accepting the *impermanence* of prompting means:

Being flexible: Being ready to change our prompts, our strategies, our approach, in response to changes in AI and the context.

Being adaptable: Being able to use different models, different techniques, different prompting styles, depending on the needs.

Being open to change: Not being afraid to experiment, to try new paths, to step outside our comfort zone.

Being aware of the present: Focusing on the here and now, on the prompt we are formulating at this moment, without worrying too much about the past or the future.

Being patient: Accepting that prompting is a process that requires time, dedication, and many attempts.

Impermanence is not a limitation, but a characteristic of prompting. It is what makes it alive, dynamic, interesting. It is what allows us to grow, to learn, to evolve together with AI.

The Prompt as an Expression of the Present Moment: The Creative Gesture Here and Now

When we formulate a prompt, we are not only trying to get an answer from the AI. We are also expressing something of ourselves: our curiosity, our intention, our creativity, our way of seeing the world.

The prompt is a creative gesture, an act of communication that takes place in the present moment. It is not an abstract entity, separate from us, but a formalized extension of our thought, our word, our imagination.

Considering the prompt as an expression of the present moment means:

Being aware of our mental state: Paying attention to our emotions, our thoughts, our sensations, while we formulate the prompt.

Being authentic: Expressing our true intention, without trying to manipulate the AI or to obtain a result at all costs.

Being present: Focusing on the prompting process, without letting ourselves be distracted by worries, expectations, or judgments.

Being free: Letting go of the need for control, the fear of making mistakes, the anxiety of perfection.

Being creative: Using prompting as an opportunity to explore new ideas, to express our imagination, to shape our vision of the world, and to change it.

Prompting, in this sense, becomes a meditative practice, a way to connect with ourselves in an authentic and meaningful dialogue.

Open Ending: Your Prompt, Your Way

There is no conclusion to this journey in the world of prompting. There are no certain answers, there are no magic formulas, there are no universal recipes.

There is, instead, an invitation to personal reflection. An invitation to consider prompting not only as a technique, but as a practice, a path, an expression of oneself.

I invite you, therefore, to ask yourself some questions:

- What is your relationship with prompting? What does it mean to you?

- What are your objectives, your aspirations, your values in prompting?

- What is your way of experimenting, of learning, of growing in prompting?

- What is your contribution to the community of prompters, to the evolution of AI, to the future of the world?

Do not seek immediate or definitive answers. Let these questions resonate within you, accompany you on your journey, inspire you to new explorations.

Let us repeat it together one last time: the perfect prompt does not exist. *Your* prompt exists, the one you create here and now, with your intention, your creativity, your awareness. A prompt that is always perfectible, always modifiable, always open to new possibilities.

And so, what is your next prompt?

Glossary Of Key Terms

Here is a glossary of the most important terms that emerged in this conversation on the art of prompting, with brief definitions for each:

Prompt: The textual (or multimodal) input provided to a language model to generate a response. It is the "question" we ask the artificial intelligence.

Prompting: The art and technique of formulating effective prompts to obtain desired results from a language model.

Prompt Engineering/Design: Terms (in this context, used interchangeably) that indicate the structured design of prompts.

Language Model: An artificial intelligence system trained on enormous amounts of textual data, capable of understanding and generating natural language.

Artificial Intelligence (IA): The discipline that deals with creating machines capable of performing tasks that normally require human intelligence, such as learning, reasoning, understanding language, and generating creative content.

Output: The response generated by the language model in response to a prompt. It can be text, code, an image, a video, or other formats.

Koan: A paradoxical question or phrase, used in the Zen tradition to stimulate intuition and overcome logical-rational thinking. In this context, used as a starting point for reflection on the themes of prompting.

Clarity (in prompting): The quality of a prompt that is formulated in a precise, unambiguous, and easily understandable way for the language model.

Intention (in prompting): The purpose or objective that one wants to achieve with a prompt. What you want the AI to do or produce.

Role Prompting: A technique that consists of instructing the AI to assume a specific role (e.g., "You are a marketing expert...") to influence the style, tone, and content of the response.

Context (in prompting): The set of additional information provided in the prompt to specify the format, style, tone of voice, topic, target audience, and other elements that help the AI to understand the request and to generate an appropriate response.

Context Switching (in prompting): A technique that consists of providing the AI with sophisticated prompts, which fully exploit the AI's ability to manage complex information and to adapt to different contexts, maintaining logical coherence.

Chain-of-Thought Prompting: A technique that consists of providing the AI with a series of logically connected prompts, in which the output of one prompt becomes the input of the next.

Parameters (of a language model): Values that control the behavior of the language model during text generation. Examples: temperature, top_p, top_k, frequency penalty, presence penalty.

Temperature: A parameter that controls the randomness or creativity of the response. Low values produce more coherent and predictable responses, high values more varied and surprising responses.

Top_p (Nucleus Sampling): A parameter that controls the variety of words considered by the AI during text generation. Low values limit the choice to the most probable words, high values allow considering also less probable words.

Top_k: a parameter that similarly limits the choice, considering only the k most probable words.

Frequency Penalty and Presence Penalty: parameters that limit the repetition, respectively, of words, or concepts.

Iteration (in prompting): The process of repeatedly modifying and refining a prompt based on the responses generated by the AI, in order to gradually improve the result.

Bias (in the context of AI): Prejudices, stereotypes, or discrimination present in the AI's training data, which can be reproduced and amplified in the model's responses.

Multimodal Prompt: A prompt that combines textual and visual input (e.g., an image and a textual description).

Serendipity: The discovery of something valuable or pleasant while looking for something else. Applied to prompting, it refers to the possibility of obtaining unexpected and useful results from the AI.

Feedback Loop: the cycle of learning and correction, in the interaction with AI.

Hallucination (of AI): A term that indicates when an AI model generates false, invented, or meaningless information, presenting it as if it were true.

Reverse engineering (in the context of prompting): process that, starting from a given text, tries to reconstruct the steps, the instructions and the prompts that could have generated it.

This glossary provides a basis for understanding the key terms discussed in this guide to prompting. However, the field of AI is constantly evolving, and new terms and concepts are constantly emerging.

ABOUT THE AUTHOR

Roberto Sammarchi

Is an Italian lawyer specializing in information law, digital communication, and personal data protection, with a qualification conferred by the National Bar Council. After graduating in Law with a thesis in computational linguistics, he earned a doctorate in Analysis and Design of Information Systems. For nearly forty years, he has dedicated himself to the complex relationship between regulations and digital technology, collaborating with companies and organizations as a consultant and interim manager. He lectures on legal responsibilities and legal aspects in the Second Level Master's Degree in Clinical Engineering at the University of Bologna.

www.ingramcontent.com/pod-product-compliance
Lightning Source LLC
LaVergne TN
LVHW041217050326
832903LV00021B/670